Praise for Bernadette Geyer

"The true ghost of *What Haunts Me* is a kind of pre-haunting, an elegy of anticipatory grief propelled as much by a poet's urgency to 'witness radiance as it happens' as by a woman's desire—as daughter, teacher, wife, mother—to document her family's life and lineage. 'It took years,' she says, 'to appreciate/ the preservation process,' the 'faint popping' of jars like 'airless metallic kisses.' This collection sweeps across geography and time: from childhood in a small steel-plant town to adulthood traveling through Europe, all while reckoning with mortality. After a loss, we are tasked with sorting through the 'tchotchke spirits' left behind. But the idea of inheritance is here more often attuned to Geyer's larger awareness of our human connectedness with the natural world. Like a red fox encountered herein, whose 'gaze contained the history of the woods,' the poems in *What Haunts Me* offer an unexpected solace, a talisman against the specter of forgetting."
— Cynthia Marie Hoffman, author of *Exploding Head*

"*What Haunts Me* travels the map of personal history through a series of immersive, quietly stunning journeys. 'We took the shortcut to our cousin's/funeral, up the steep road to Port Vue,//' recalls the poem, 'Dead Men,' 'past houses staggered like thumbtacks/between the narrow lane and the hillside.' Bernadette Geyer's collection observes labor in all shapes and forms, and breaks through to understanding of how our loves, joys, and griefs must be understood as part of a larger moment in time and place. We do this to better prepare us for dialogue with our own children; we do this, metaphorically and literally, to better pass along our

name. But this book's weighty cloth of intent is worn lightly thanks to the poet's dry humor and gift for the lyric stitch—'Remembering is quick and sharp as a stumble,/unexpected as a fly/or a flurry of moonlight.' These poems are full of beautiful surprises."
— Sandra Beasley, author of *Made to Explode: Poems*

"Bernadette Geyer's *What Haunts Me* is the apt title for a book where the past hallows the present tense. Times before jobs lost, between the good times and between economic hardships. These are poems of place and family, American as a backyard pond full of Koi. Reflections on Angkor Wat, the ruins of home, and a rundown steel town past its days. There is so much of human labor here: glassblowers and Ugandan beekeepers, of funerals and family dinners, and dig downs into ancestry on the level of names. This is a book of poems that will haunt you with the lives it narrates long after you have read the last page."
— Sean Thomas Dougherty, author of *Death Prefers the Minor Keys*

What Haunts Me

Bernadette Geyer

APRIL GLOAMING

Publisher's Cataloguing-in-Publication Data

Geyer, Bernadette
    What haunts me / written by Bernadette Geyer
    ISBN: 978-1-953932-39-6

1. Poetry: General 2. Poetry: Women 3. Poetry: Southern Gothic
I. Title II. Author

Library of Congress Control Number: 2025943889

For Peter and Frida

Contents

Contents

Kinship

The koi thread underwater paths, steer
themselves beneath one, then another, of the fountains—

domesticated within the confines of the concrete pond.
The gray-green water reflects a glass-and-steel sky.

Their razored fins barely surface as they slip through
small maelstroms of bubbles, sloughing their spines

to reveal gold-orange flash and milky tumescence.
What have we done to deserve this kinship with fish?

Do we all simply multiply and divide, savoring
the whirlpool jet spray on our taut backs, surfacing

now and again amid the froth of a cunning heaven?
How can we tell the koi we know, we understand?

I am descended from fish. My ancestors
are ghost javelins—their lithe bodies a promise.

Sometimes I Damn These Hands

Sometimes I damn these hands:
their need to chop and pluck and prune.
I damn the glow I get as I heave
the bag of leaves onto my shoulder.

Sometimes I see my parents' hands
instead—the lines, the scars, the way
their fingers grasped the trowels.
Sometimes I damn the cramp

from pinching weeds out at the root.
I damn my spine its evening groans,
and when I wake to a cloudless dawn,
only the memory of pain remains.

Sometimes, I damn the calling,
this gift that courses through me,
warming these damned hands within
the stiffened canvas of their gloves.

Bernadette Geyer

Thanksgiving

When times were good,
our mother bought extra hearts
for the turkey neck soup,
the largest carrot from the garden

a shock of orange in the broth,
fat glinting on the surface
hinting at more, the troth
of wealth ladled among us.

The year our father was laid off,
we savored the neck bone
and deemed it enough
as the lone carrot shone

bright on the center plate.
That neck would yield no excess.
We hunted and pecked for meat,
one heart portioned among us.

Heat Lightning

The nights it happened, we'd set up chairs
in the back yard, watch the skies

instead of the black & white TV handed
down from our grandfather when he upgraded

to a console. We bugged our eyes as wide
as we could, tried hard not to blink

for fear we'd miss one of the flashes
outlining the clouds that separated

us from the stars, the clouds that acted as a screen
against which we could watch this display

of nature's fireworks. Silly as pups, we tried
to predict where the light would flare next—

looked there instead of where the flash
last occurred, because we'd been told

that lightning never strikes the same place
twice. Even now, I find it just as hard

to witness radiance as it happens,
just as hard to stop myself from trying.

Bernadette Geyer

Portrait of My Father Looking for Four-Leaf Clovers

Abroad for the first time, far
from the siren call of his workroom,
my father idles in a close-cropped field
within the ragged towered walls
of Pevensey Castle. His calloused fingertips
graze clovers instead of clutching sandpaper
or guiding a table saw to rip the length of a board.

I haven't done this since I was a kid,
he says, and I can only believe it—having grown
used to the sight of him always weeding
and watering, hammering and sanding,
tasked with a vast array of things waiting
to be transformed by his hands.

No, my father was not accustomed
to the horizonless ocean of free time
he now faced in this country to which I
have brought him and my mother.

In four months, this man who leans
into the field with the weight of his years
will have his first heart attack. This moment
a prelude to the leisure and lassitude
he would soon be forced to endure
in the name of recuperation.

What Haunts Me

What I want to say is this:
for 55 years my father looked at clovers
as something to be eradicated from the lawn,
a blight, a pox, a nuisance.

The truth is that my father
never found a four-leaf clover
in that field—
but that wasn't the reason he sat there
and looked for a while.

Bernadette Geyer

Distortion

I can tell this photo was once smaller
by the blur of distortion
that comes from making a thing much larger
than it is naturally meant to be.

Side-saddle on a motorcycle,
in the black jeans you studded yourself,
you smile at a camera held by hands
that could have been your first husband's,

or your second's, or the hands
of the man we called Grandpa.
I can tell this is you, though the image
is not one easily reconciled

with the grandmother who sends
my birthday cards early—
Because you just never know...
And you begin to allow more of your past

to slip into conversation, blurring
the sharp edges of reality until it is as unclear
as this picture, which reveals no truth
greater than the fact of your existence.

Lessons

In the blue womb of the living room chair,
Mom's eyes flutter closed. Her mouth
falls open, as does the medical textbook
in her lap, displaying photos of a dissected

fetal pig, its heart and liver
like rough-hewn garnets within its body.
Dad tosses popcorn into the air, by turns missing
her mouth and his own, as my sisters and I

vacillate between giggling and begging him to stop.
Another kernel falls next to him on the sofa.
He picks it up and eats it anyway, grinning.
Our bodies are so embarrassing to us.

He illustrates the humor of the self the way
no textbook ever could. Look!—see how we
falter and stumble with our funny bones,
laughter swimming through our silly veins.

Bernadette Geyer

Complicit

Not often, but
sometimes—

knowing it wrong
yet drawn

to lift as if
to lift a veil—

I raised the bedskirts
in my parents' room

to see the gleam
of the chamber

stowed in theirs.
Not often, but

sometimes—I
dared to look.

Hunting

For years, my father busied himself with his knife,
as distant deer passed just beyond his range of vision—
until the day he looked up with time enough
to trade knife for gun, take aim, and fire, dropping
the deer deep in the woods.

Across the hills, he hollered to Uncle Bill, who
never mocked the days another wood carving
was all my father had to show for his day's hunting—
men for whom hope and ritual were enough.

My father dragged that deer to a clearing to gut it,
novice fingers unaware of the need to pinch off
the buck's esophagus before slicing through.
Strangers rushed to find the source of all the shouting,
this man covered in blood that was not his.

It would be years before another kill.
Time enough to perfect technique
as he whittled away the hours,
his blade sharp
and ready.

Bernadette Geyer

The Hunter's Privilege

Our locked eyes stopped
the ticking seconds—he in the thicket,

I on the trail, arrested in our paths.
When he glanced away, his profile,

with its pointed snout, confirmed
my thought: red fox.

I was not close enough to discern
the shadow ripple of muscle in his haunch,

though I presumed it was there
from his steady stance, his tensed stillness.

His gaze contained the history of the woods,
memories of every hunger, every meal

he'd lucked into. Eyes of caution
and longing, poised to attack or flee

with equal readiness. His swift feet knew
from experience the exact trajectory

of every escape route
from every square inch of this terrain.

What Haunts Me

I wondered what he thought of me,
weak animal that I am, the instincts

of my lineage wasted on my generation.
Here I was, with the hunter's privilege,

animal meeting animal in its element.
We let each other go, the fox and I,

neither of us knowing which was hunter,
which was prey. A breeze filtered

through the woods to rouse the second-hand
from its slumber. Sound returned—

the crunching of leaves
dead beneath my moving feet.

Bernadette Geyer

An Idyllic Small Town, Circa 1970s

That was back before Dad lost his job.
Before Mom went back to school. Back when
we had all four grandparents and none of us girls
was old enough to want boyfriends. Back
when *husband* was a word we snuck glances at
in the "adult" books in the library. Before
the library was shut down because the posse
of volunteers from the ladies' club diminished
in ranks as well as stature. Before they gave away
every damn book on those shelves. Of course,
that was also back before I ever dreamed
I'd call myself a writer. Back when I could still
cartwheel across Grandma's front lawn,
stopping only to wave at my parents as they sat
in their car, waiting in line to fill up their tank
with scarce, expensive, $2-per-gallon gasoline.
Back when electric cars were considered
mere science fiction. Before science fiction
turned into *Hey, that shit could really happen!*
Back when Cooter was fixing the General Lee
and Dirty Harry played chauffeur to an orangutan.
Back before all those actors and singers became
politicians. Back in the before-times—those
half-dreamed fictions stitched together
as one Frankenstein memory of my childhood.

What Haunts Me

False Light

A fist of flame pierces the air above the valley,
flaring the gases of the Irvin Works plant.

The sulfurous stench that assaults my senses opens
shop doors and bank accounts here. The smell of work.

Fresh air means unemployment, means hand-me-downs,
means government cheese and a lean winter. For decades

I have watched the smoke billow overhead, substantial
and constant as a demon. Below, in this valley

cut through by the river, barges deliver coal north
from the mines, deliver slag south from the belching

mouths of the mills to form new hills. A solemn train
groans hello and goodbye to the itinerant barge that winks

its red eye, its green eye—the reflections do-si-do the moon
on the water. I find even this false light a pleasing one.

Bernadette Geyer

Pond

—for Eric

The goldfish swim in circles,
seemingly oblivious to the cat
whose eyes miss nothing—
not even the merest of ripples
beneath the surface of the pond.

Dragonflies alight in pairs
on the water lily, a respite
from the sun and humidity.
You watch and learn—botany,
entomology—life is learning,
all the seasonal world a classroom.

Only a breeze stirs the thin film
of algae that struggles into autumn.
By the time its traces have faded,
you will have brought the fish
inside for the winter. The cat

will search out other distractions.

Whatever Saves Us Is Sacred

—for the swans

Oh Petra, I could write the expected poem
to you, about how love chooses us, not we
it. But you would know this already.

When you first sighted that grand bird,
did you suspect? Or when he drifted
like a hushed psalm beside you, did you

consider him a sage who needed no speech—
not even the vocabulary of swans,
translatable only by sun and pond?

Petra, I could say that we are always
betraying ourselves: either we
close our eyes and point, or we take

only what we are given. But not you.
If your great lineage ends with you,
if your ancestors look down upon you

with pity or revulsion, at least you
will have experienced the security of belief
few of us will ever realize is possible.

And the swan paddle boat you loved
will drift on, propelled by water, faith,
and everything that ever saves us.

Preservation

i.

My daughter hopscotches between giddy
anticipation and weeping at the empty space
where her crib-turned-daybed used to be.
I am pickling beets, waiting for her new bed
to arrive. Boiled beet in hand, I slough the skin
from it with my thumbs, my fingers stained
with a shocking red that washes easily away,
considering the root's historic use as a dye.

I rough cut the beets into chunks, pour
the pickling fluid over them. A whiff
of the vinegar-mustard mix brings back
the sting in my eyes and nostrils every fall
that my parents jarred dozens of quarts
of pepper rings. It took years for me to appreciate
the preservation process—from the hours
of preparation, sterilizing jars in the sweat lodge
of the kitchen, to the cool-down period that ended
with the sign of an assured vacuum seal:
the faint popping of airless metallic kisses.

ii.

In the re-created Powhatan Village in Jamestown,
deerskins are stretched out to dry, cords pulling
the pelts taut within their tree branch hewn frames.
Oyster shells fill crude wooden bowls
so visitors can use the shells' jagged edges
to grasp the time and effort it took to scrape
the fur from what would one day become
a papoose or quiver. My daughter and I clutch
our shells, angle the sharpest edges against
the skin and drag hard, shaving only a few wisps
at a time. She gives up quickly, but I am stubborn.
I want to see progress. With each pass I make,
my shell presses hard into the palm of my hand,
an impression that lingers even as we move on
to other exhibits in the village. The sour-rotten
smell of weathered hide follows us all day,
bits of fur clinging to our clothes.

What Haunts Me

iii.

Frank once told me every animal has enough
brain matter to tan its own hide, the emulsified
oils superior to the chemicals used in modern
processes. He showed me the tobacco bag he'd
made from an otter pelt, explained how he used
it to hold Mishma, an herbal blend of tobacco
used in ceremonial pipes. I think he may have
expected me to cringe, or pull my hand away.
But I'd been on a hunt before, learned how to spot
the trampled leaves where a deer had bedded,
to follow tracks, to wait. I'd fingered the velvet
of a dead deer's skull cap, and then the smooth
bone after weeks of brining so that my father
could mount the antlers to display. I held
Frank's tobacco bag to my nose, inhaled
the heady mixture of herb and leather,
the pungent scent of death and utility.

iv.

Not a single pane of stained glass remained unbroken
in the building folks still referred to as St. Cecilia's—
despite its closure as a school and church nearly twenty
years before—the building now marked for demolition
as just one more blight in a town whose residents are
no longer surprised when abandoned houses seem
to self-immolate to escape fate's wrecking ball. I presume
the ghost in the storage room above the sacristy has fled,
along with whatever traces of chalk dust may have remained
from the hours the school's children spent whacking erasers
together as punishment for using the Lord's name in vain.
After the parish closed, *beautiful dreams* for the property
died along with its new owners, the building shunted off
on the borough to become yet another burden—not enough
money to preserve it, just enough to tear it down.
In every town in every country there is someone fighting
to save something that no one else cares about, the world
full of stories that repeat stories told before. We cannot
honor every room that ever existed. How could we.

What Haunts Me

v.

Before we disassembled our daughter's daybed, we
documented it according to her wishes: one photo
of its usual disheveled state (a carelessness only children
find agreeable), another with her stuffed animals
arranged in the exacting way I have ordered my own life,
and one of her feigning sleep, a smile dimpling
the exposed side of her face, her feet
pushing at the bed's constricting frame.

Measure Twice, Cut Once

The cut string retains
the memory of the whole.
Unravel it.

Feel it between
your fingers,
this innocuous thread.

This tether, this strand
that seams a cuff
to its sleeve.

This puller of teeth,
this floss, this kin
to hair in all its traits.

This hidden unifier.
This overlooked and undervalued
soldier's staple.

This mender of wounds.
This accomplice
to thieves and healers.

What Haunts Me

Yes, this thread. This
bedding of birds.
Unravel it from its spool.

Substantial
as a sliver of glass
between your fingers.

Bernadette Geyer

Long Before You See Them You Hear Them

their great distant hubbub, urgent chatter,
a choral round of squawks. You scan the sky,
but trees and houses shield the distant horizon.

As you work to clear winter's detritus
from your grass, the din spreads and nears
until, at last, their sloppy V appears.

Actually, more of a W as flocks merge
and fuse, only to re-fracture against
the steel gray of this nascent Spring sky.

They race the rain, stay mere wing-beats
ahead, ride the crest of the front
like surfers of an invisible sea.

Now overhead, their noise masks
the grind of the neighbor's chainsaw.
They are that loud. You would swear

it seemed the world ceased its progress
to tip its massive head up to watch
as that parade of prodigal sons passed.

And when the caws of the jealous crows
replaced the ruckus of the geese,
you imagined your own way of returning.

Before the Blessing

I would lie still,
trying not to hear the walls
and their sepia whispers,
my face turned
into the pillow to avoid
smelling the oak breath
of the house
flaunting its speakeasy past.

The shifting joint of wall
and ceiling chanted my name
as attic crawl spaces
knocked their way
into my dreams,
waking me
with their persistence.

On my way downstairs,
the wooden banister
clutched at my wrist,
an old woman hissing:
Listen to my story.

Bernadette Geyer

A Failed Romanticism

i.

The roots of silk cotton trees
draped the slumberous doorways
of Angkor Wat's Ta Prohm temple,
and for a while the photogenic ruins
were left that way for the sake
of tourists eager to outdo each other
in the framing and commodification
of the sublime. Ruin is, after all,
in the eyes of the beholder.
In this case, the scholars who,
as a *concession to the general taste*
for the picturesque deemed Ta Prohm
the temple *best merged with the jungle,*
but not yet to the point of becoming a part of it.
Neither nature nor man having bested the other
in this perfect example. And so it was saved
from further deterioration,
preserved in figurative amber.

What Haunts Me

ii.

When we selected the 800-year-old
Woodspring Priory for our summer vacation,
we told the children it was a castle.
And to them, it just as well could have been,
perception being everything when you are young.
Priory to farmhouse. Farmhouse to ruin.
Ruin to holiday rental for two families with kids.

Nothing that lives so long can expect
to retain a single identity. I myself
have been *daughter, teacher, wife, mother.*

Grazed by our careless shoulders,
the narrow plastered halls in the Priory
chipped further, ghosting our sleeves.
Our midnight trips to the kitchen
further challenged by the uneven treads
of the helixed stone stairwells.
And we relished it all, photographed ourselves
against the backdrop of crumbling walls
that once defined a cloister, winced
as the low lintels struck and left on our foreheads
impressions that we'd recount for years.

iii.

But to prove not all shambles are so revered—
so pictorial and preserved—the Wagon Wheel Bar
disappeared a mere twelve years after it closed,
after it had served as the ruin to many,
become ruin itself, the surrounding trees and brush
unrepentant in their creep and slither.

We'd grown used to the sight of the bar's
apologetic slump against the eroding hillside
across the river from the Clairton Steel Works—
landmarks we passed on the way to the home
of my childhood. It is likely that no one
had ever called it *picturesque,* though perhaps
at closing time the view of the mill lights
reflected on the river beyond the parking lot
and across the train tracks gave patrons the impression
of a world turned topsy-turvy so that the coal
and slag barges could slumber among the stars.

What Haunts Me

iv.

Once, I imagined returning to our own version
of Angkor Wat—our grass gone un-mown and ivy
lewdly fingering the brick and siding of our
temporarily abandoned home, finally reclaimed
by the woods that were razed in the 1960s
for this development of split levels
and mock colonials, cul-de-sacs and carports.

On the plane ride home, I'd wondered
what insects we'd find colonizing the corners
of our pantry shelves, the ants at last
discovering the honey I'd bought to sweeten
my bitter brews. Could I come to love
this home and embrace its shortcomings
the way I'd made peace with the cold
Castello de Montegufoni I thought would
provide inspiration for my writing one summer,
accept the gaps in our bricks' crumbling mortar
the way I'd accepted the splintered wood shutter
I'd used to keep out the Tuscan night?

Bernadette Geyer

It was August: when what has been abandoned
falls prey to whatever has learned to survive
despite itself—the crabgrass that crab-walks its way
across what's left when the parched lawn
gives itself up as a grey-brown ash blown
into the panting tongues of sedum leaves, a dust
the scant rains of late summer can't wash off.

And while a part of me knew we'd been on vacation
for only two weeks, and that the pest control guy
was scheduled to come the first Friday we were away,
and the lawn guys on the Friday after that,
there was a deeper part of me that wanted
to return to ruin, that wanted to know
the magnitude of the necessity of our daily presence.

What Haunts Me

v.

This house whose walls we skimcoat and paint,
whose fence we mend and whose mortar we seal—
whose photographed *before* we meticulously place beside
its corresponding and utterly improved *after.*

Bernadette Geyer

The Long Man

i.

The monk gazes from his priory window
at the chalk hill, sloped away from the brambled field

beside the road. In this chapel, across the vaulted,
gap-toothed wood of the attic above the kitchen,

he prays in the company of doves that roost
in lichen-yellow belfries, as close to their God

as he can get, wingless as he is in his dun-colored robe,
knotted rope dangling at his bent knee.

The monk's rote prayers echo against the walls, filling
the cracks of the plaster like doubting fingers pressed

into wounds. After years of questions without response,
a man will sometimes form his own answer. A room

can hold only so much emptiness: the monk rises,
leaves the priory while his brothers sleep.

What Haunts Me

ii.

The farmers noticed it first, in certain slants of light
against the hillside: the figure of a giant carved into the chalk

just beneath the scrub and grass, a pattern no ruminant
in its grazing could make. They affixed him there permanently

with yellow bricks, not knowing what idle hands, unclasped
from their forsaken prayers, made this Long Man.

God or pilgrim, he stands there still, and I have traveled far
to see him as the monk meant him to be seen, from a bedroom

that once was a chapel. At night, my eyes seek out
the Long Man's moonlit presence on the hillside,

perfectly framed by the priory window. My husband's
light snores echo off the chipped plaster walls.

Doves sleep in the belfry ruins, their pale bodies like hands
pressed together in a silent *Amen*. I pray—for blind faith—

to the Long Man, to the lonely chalk-smeared hands
that fashioned him. A room can hold only so much

emptiness, especially when the night is this quiet,
and your god has stopped talking to you.

Bernadette Geyer

For a Taxi Driver Named Comfort

—Las Vegas 1997

Is she still there—her taxi reeking
of pine-scented air freshener—trawling
the Strip for fares as the sun retires
to let the neon glow take over its shift?

Is she still there, who ferried me through
that strange prosthetic town, and why is it
after all these years I should remember
so well her broad shoulders hunched

in her tense gripping of the steering wheel,
her deep voice burdened with knowledge?
Despite dozens of cities, countless drivers
since, despite the roads I've propelled myself

along, why is it her to whom I offer this
humble gesture of remembrance, and why
do I pray for her who simply carried me
when my blistered, unsteady feet could not?

What Barbara Told Us

She waited until we finished
our self-guided tour of the husks

of buildings that endured
in the former Warsaw Ghetto.

She waited until we had shot
our fill of photographs, switched out

rolls of film. Our steps were snared
in the viscous spell of history when she

began to speak: *It was never a moral
question—bribery and stealing. If*

*the Polish stole, it was from the Russians,
or the Germans, or the Austro-Hungarians.*

*If the government was cheated,
that was okay, because it wasn't theirs.*

She offered this not as apology
or excuse, but fact, just as

the bullet-pocked wall would never
apologize for its blemishes

as we skimmed our fingertips
over its marred, but proud, skin.

Reading Lips

I try not to stare at the man sleeping
across the aisle from me, whose body slowly melts
into his ankles with age. Eyes closed,
his mouth and tongue move in silent,

dreamy flutterings. I use my peripheral vision,
but am increasingly desperate to know
what dreams puzzle his mind, what words
he tries to form with those slackened lips—

those words that may, in fact, be the truth we feel
so close to in sleep, that truth we wake with
in our mouths, that slumbers on the tips of our tongues,
but lingers behind as we slowly emerge

into consciousness. The truth we wish someone
could translate for us while we sleep,
mouthing the air in silent prayers.
That truth I know he knows, but doesn't realize.

Bernadette Geyer

White House Plumber, 27 Years

A smile devoid of irony, you grin
with lips unused to parting in delight,

hidden so long beneath
your voluminous but well-kept moustache.

You are happy: eyes narrowed
to slivers, the skin at their corners

radiating in laugh lines. A crisp button front shirt
you'd never wear on the job.

Your photograph hangs beside
the Head Storekeeper of 46 years, above

the Florist of 18. Immortalized here,
on your elbow, beneath the porcelain sink,

head close to the bend just where the pipe
enters the wall. Did you go home that evening,

pull your wife close, inhale with gratitude
the scent of her hair just where it tucks

behind her ear? Did you ask yourself
Now will they see me as she sees me?

What Haunts Me

Oh, to finally be recognized for your worth—
with this photo, catching tourist eyes

in the White House Visitors' Center,
on the same wall as the Engineering Foreman

of 41 years, the Assistant Usher of 16.
Though none so prominently placed

as the Doorman of 46 years: shown poised
near the front door, along with the President's

dog, both heads angled toward the unseen
that approaches from beyond the radiant

geometry of the opened door, from beyond
the frame of the photograph. Master, mistress,

any comers to validate their calling.

Glassblower

Passed down through centuries, the tools remain
the same—their use adapted for more modern
tastes. The blowpipe pulls a gather of
the molten glass; the gaffer spins it as

he blows to form the parison—a bubble—
rolled in bits of colored glass, then marvered
to a simple shape against a carbon
paddle or a metal plate. A breath

into the pipe: the piece becomes a vase,
a pretty thing. Using the calipers,
he elongates the glass, as gravity

takes hold to arc the pull. This swan-necked vase
will fit a single bud. Impractical,
its beauty is desired nonetheless.

Bernadette Geyer

My Inheritance

When a Chiga beekeeper dies in Uganda,
his eldest son receives a small model beehive
as a sign that he has inherited his father's
power over the bees. The crude vessels

that represent my inheritance are
cardboard boxes stacked like hive cells
in my parents' attic, basement, and garage.
Even they don't know what many of the boxes

hold, some dating back to before
our family's move from a cramped duplex
to the house I left after college. Sometimes
an artifact escapes "the archive" and makes its way

to me—stowed away in a care package
or birthday gift—wrapped casually
in decades-old newspaper. One year,
it was an Indian-head penny the size of

a pie pan. Then, a clear vinyl umbrella I used
when I was eight. Remembrances trapped
in the amber of their own uselessness.
But what my sisters and I fear most is

What Haunts Me

the inevitable ceremony to come: the months
to be spent opening box upon box,
three Pandoras releasing back into the world
swarms of tchotchke spirits. How can we

refuse their wish to leave behind
this archive of us? Can we instead beg them
to sell the house, pay off their debts
and live well while they can?

Acrostic: Dolores

Dark fish wriggles free from the lake
Of her mother's body, gasps in
Luminous air. White-gloved hands
Open to catch her, channel her to safety,
Rock her as the mother's body turns on itself,
Eclamptic. Her name bestowed on her in a
Sigh. A yoke. A memento. A curse.

What Haunts Me

Dead Men

We took the shortcut to our cousin's
funeral, up the steep road to Port Vue,

past houses staggered like thumbtacks
between the narrow lane and the hillside.

Only the retaining walls kept the yards
from spilling into the street during storms.

The Morse code of wooden dots and dashes
flashed by as our father explained the dead men,

how their placement—perpendicular
to the ones we could see from the street—

would give stability. All that earth
pressing right through them.

The Visitation

The dough is getting sticky, so my mother
adds more flour and works it
with her grandmother's rolling pin
on her grandmother's wooden baker's board.

She rolls a length of dough, cuts it
with the rim of an overturned bowl,
sees how many rounds
she'll be able to fit this time.

She piles the trimmed excess on the side
to be used in the next batch, reincarnated
repeatedly until there remains
only one bowl's circumference worth.

I have witnessed this so many times,
I don't have to be there to know
this is exactly how it would have happened.
There would have first been the rhythm—

thud, out, in, lift, thud, out, in, lift—
of the rolling pin. And then the words
that went with the song that went with the rhythm
would have gradually made their presence

known, quietly at first, like the mantra of violets,
then louder, until she realized she had been
singing all along, in Hungarian, the tune
her father sang while working in his cellar,

marking in pencil on the heating ducts
the dates of the first frost, the last onion.

> *Az a szép, az a szép,*
> *akinek a szeme kék . . .*

She spoons the warm potato and cheese mixture
into the center of the dough rounds, folds them
and pinches the edges, while she tells her father
what a great year we've had. She forgets
the snow outside, my father in the living room. She is
making the pierogis for Christmas Eve, singing
Az a szép with her father, who didn't have to be there
to know this is exactly how it would have happened.

Bernadette Geyer

Ash Wednesday

I don't need to be told—
today, of all days—that I

am dust and that to dust
I shall return. Of course.

And in the midst of grief
over the inevitable death

of a housecat, I lift
my forehead to an ashen thumb.

My prayers take the form
of anticipation. With or without.

I can do this. The sky
bruises above me as I bear

the full weight of keeping
so many promises. My days

holy with obligations. I
cannot do this. One week

since the first signs of illness.
The wild jaundice of the cat's

eyes as the doctor slipped
the needle in. It eats now.

Pisses, too. I offer burnt
clichés to my daughter. I

can do this. I feed the cat.
Ash stains my fingers.

Bernadette Geyer

Explaining Cremation to Our Daughter
at the Dinner Table

i.

We explained the fire
and what it leaves behind.

ii.

I don't even remember
how the subject of the cat's ashes
came up, how we still needed
to figure out what to do with them.
As she reached for her milk,
our daughter said she wanted
to see the box
that held what remained.

What Haunts Me

iii.

In *Paradise Lost*,
when the Archangel's sword
struck Lucifer, Milton wrote
"then Satan first knew pain."
That terrible thing: first knowledge.
That burden. And now, as parents,
my husband and I are tasked
to pass down these burdens
to our daughter.

iv.

That day
she didn't understand
until she had searched the house
herself, poked her doubting fingers
into the wounds left behind,
and finally understood that he
was not there, would never again
be there. She threw herself
onto the sofa and sobbed,
refusing to look at me
as I set my hand on her back—
as if it could draw the grief away.
As if I had room to accept it.

Bernadette Geyer

v.

What it comes down to
is how soon we each fall
from ignorance.

vi.

There are days when I curse
Schröedinger, because now,
every time I look at that box
on my office shelf—its polished
sheen and gold engraving—
I know. Dammit. I know.

His Inheritance

It took them one weekend to clear
their father's small house of the things
that remained to testify that he
had been there, in Old Orchard Beach.

My husband and his sister sorted
their inheritance in musty silence.
Most of it—newspaper and magazine
clippings, old bills—had already

been tossed by their father's friend.
Only his brother's knife from Iwojima,
some photos, and his writings remained.
The house of his self built with pen

and paper, vast and borderless, antithesis
of the wood-paneled two-room cottage
he rented because it was near the ocean
and because he knew some people there.

When my husband returned, he brought
his inheritance—the taped-up box
that sulked in the basement for years,
long enough that its presence

went unnoticed most days, until one of us
needed something from the box beneath it,
or the box behind it, and we
were obligated to wrestle with its heft,

until the year we uprooted ourselves,
passed on the box to his sister.
Except for the knife. You can use a knife.

Bernadette Geyer

Remembering Is Short

Remembering is quick and sharp as a stumble,
unexpected as a fly
                  or flurry of moonlight.

Remembering is a swift kick in the groin,
the tang of an apple
                  or stipple of firefly light.

Remembering is the glimpse of a woman's breast
or the slip of a blade,
                  fleeting and intangible as a wink.

But forgetting—
forgetting is a dead star whose light
                  we continue to see.

The Eye Forgets

Geometry's the first to go—
its menagerie of forms shifts
to the tactile realm
of corners and curves.

Color is translated into
smell—how orange
quickens the nose
while berry blues seep their salve

into gasping pores.
Light follows and the eye
forgets morning and night—
despondent moon and weightless sun

arrive/depart to little fanfare.
The eye forgets the self,
forgets mirrors.
Eye forgets that sky

and earth do not overlap,
forgets that once
it was considered so
important (its functions

deftly assumed
by the other senses).
The eye forgets it exists
and so, it closes.

The Foot Remembers Its Favorite Shoe

It was an open-toed
rust-orange wedge
that hissed when passing
the other girls at school.

Thinking back
to that virgin exposition—
that first time pink polish
shone out from under

a steel-and-wood desk
too low for legs
to cross and uncross,
the foot remembers

wanting to dangle
carelessly, seductively,
wanting to *clack clack*
that heel all day

up and down the holy halls
of St. Cecilia's junior high.
The foot sighs, flexes.
Sinful, naked foot.

Naming the Bones

It was simple at first:
we named them
as we broke them—
radius and ulna, tibia
and fibula—names

like celestial bodies.
We searched the sky
hoping to see
our phalanges and femurs
poised alongside

Orion and Cassiopeia.
We bruised our bones
to make them stronger,
striving to shape and mold
our bodies to our will.

Experience taught us
the green twig may fracture
incompletely
but the damage
can never be undone.

Alzheimers

i.

A vast beach
where each word
written in the sand
      erases the one
           before it.
"Shell" becomes "hand,"
"stranger" replaces "husband."

ii.

Aunt Mary and Uncle Steve
danced together
at the nursing home,
marking their 50th anniversary.
While he held her
           close,
she whispered—
My skylark,
    my starfish,
       my stranger.

Ksiazek

i.

It could've evolved
from the Polish word for "prince"—
Książę—and yet it was just as close
to the spelling for "book"—*Książka*
—though elsewhere it was rumored
to derive from the term for "illicit
son of a priest"—*Ksiądzek*.

ii.

There was never an attempt
by my father's ancestors
to ease the burden of pronunciation
or assimilate in the way the Molnars
on my mother's side became Millers
and her great-Aunt Julia Barsse
became Bass when she left Belgium
for a farm in Ohio. No, the Ksiazeks
kept the twisted tongue and ambiguity.

What Haunts Me

iii.

Pap was nicknamed "Bookie"
because he ran numbers, not
for any literary linkage. I remember
him in his rocking chair on the porch,
how he studied the daily sports scores,
checked them against the coded sheet
he unfolded when he was sure
no one was watching.

iv.

In Warsaw, the scripted blue neon
across the front of *Dom Książki* beckoned,
books stacked and racked in the window,
colorful dust jackets to draw customers
into this "House of Books."
In another district, I posed—
my hand a compass point aimed
at the sign for *Książęca* street,
"princely" street. Home
to the Warsaw Stock Exchange
and its traders who watch
the numbers, check them
against their own coded sheets.

v.

City of thin beet soup, vodka,
and everything in aspic. City
of beauty pageant contestants
with my same exaggerated teeth.
City whose name was born
from the love of a fisherman
for a mermaid. City that would later
become a sea of rubble.
City rising up. Phoenix city.

vi.

Unaware of meaning, I photographed
anything with a word resembling my name.
Bookstores, streets, even a memorial
I would later discover was placed to honor
the *Księgarzom Polskim*, "Polish booksellers,"
and others who, during the Nazi occupation,
rescued books in order to defend
and maintain their national culture.

vii.

Back in the U.S., the movie poster
in an antique shop proclaimed *Książę i żebrak*
in great gothic red letters
as two men, prince and pauper,
crossed swords with each other.
I pointed, showing my husband the word
he'd struggled to learn how to spell
the first months we were dating.

viii.

I look through my Warsaw photos,
grateful for the guide who included me
in so many of them: posed at sunset
on the Old Town wall, smiling
from a seat on the city tram,
solemn in a Ghetto doorway.
Sometimes a name is all you have
to prove you once existed.
Sometimes a photo, the only record.
Here, right here. Let me show you.

Bernadette Geyer

Ghazal

When I left there, people knew my name.
Looking back, no one ever really knew my name.

Wish me into the wolf's mouth.
When I turned 22, I outgrew my name.

I cried to learn a new language.
With old teeth, I tried to chew my name.

In the sand of the beach where an ancient bottle
Washed ashore, my daughter drew my name.

In that furniture-less house of trust,
I promised you I would not eschew my name.

We stand on the sheer ice bridge of time
While frigid winds howl through my name.

O Geier, o scavenger,
I am trying to live up to my name.

Ghost, I Remember

the rotten plum color of that carpet
in my room. Every splintercold snick

of ice under my nails as I scraped
winter from the inside of my windows.

Some days I schemed to conjure you
but then recanted while my numb

fingers fumbled a plastic rosary, pitted
one form of belief against another.

I trained my newly pierced ears to hear
night whisper its vulgar gossip

into the dusty folds of the curtains,
but refused to confirm with open eyes

any shifting shapes in the shadows.
I learned to doubt, and then I left.

At times, I return to that house
with my daughter—whose future

I am tasked to shape with knowledge
and faith but shape, instead, by my

lack of both. Ghost, there is no need now
for you to scuff and pace and ache

these loose-board floors, no need
to spook the watch hands backwards,

because now you are the least
of what, daily, haunts me.

Notes

"Whatever Saves Us Is Sacred" – In 2007, multiple news stories reported on a wild black swan named Petra that flew into a German lake and fell in love with a swan-shaped paddle boat. Petra refused to leave her "mate" even when all the other swans flew south for the winter.

"Preservation" – Italicized *beautiful dreams* in section four is from a quote by Rev. Casimir Kedzierski from "Glassport landmark St. Cecilia to be demolished," by Michael DiVittorio, *TribLIVE News*, August 27, 2011.

"A Failed Romanticism" – Italicized text in first section taken from *Angkor: A Guide to the Angkor Monuments*, by Maurice Glaize, translated by Nils Tremmel, 1997 (accessed online December 20, 2013) https://www.theangkorguide.com/text.htm.

"The Visitation" – English translation of the Hungarian song lyrics is approximately "She is pretty, she is pretty, that blue-eyed one is pretty."

"Ghazal" – *Geier* is the German word for vulture.

Acknowledgments

With special thanks and appreciation to the editors and magazines in which versions of many of these poems first appeared:

American Journal of Nursing: "Lessons"; *Arkansas Review*: "Long Before You See Them You Hear Them"; *Barn Owl Review*: "An Idyllic Small Town, Circa 1970s"; *Barrow Street*: "Ghazal"; *Beltway Poetry Quarterly*: "White House Plumber, 27 Years"; *Border Crossing*: "Whatever Saves Us Is Sacred"; *The Broadkill Review*: "Distortion"; *Cold Mountain Review*: "Ksiazek"; *Common Ground Review*: "The Long Man"; *Connecticut River Review*: "The Visitation"; *Connections*: "The Foot Remembers Its Favorite Shoe"; *Electric Literature*: "A Failed Romanticism"; *The Evansville Review*: "Remembering Is Short"; *Gargoyle*: "The Eye Forgets" and "Ghost, I Remember"; *Ilanot Review*: "Acrostic: Dolores"; *The MacGuffin*: "Complicit"; *Mid-America Poetry Review*: "Pond"; *The Paris-American*: "Thanksgiving"; *Pebble Lake Review*: "Measure Twice, Cut Once"; *The Pedestal Magazine*: "Naming the Bones"; *Permafrost*: "Alzheimers"; *Pine Hills Review*: "Hunting"; *Potomac Review*: "Before the Blessing"; *Rattle*: "Dead Men" and "Reading Lips"; *Reverie Magazine*: "His Inheritance"; *roger*: "Kinship" and "Sometimes I Damn These Hands"; *South Carolina Review*: "Explaining Cremation to Our Daughter at the Dinner Table"; *South Dakota Review*: "False Light" and "The Hunter's Privilege"; *The Sunlight Press*: "Glassblower"; *VerseWrights*: "Heat Lightning," "My Inheritance," "Portrait of My Father Looking for Four-Leaf Clovers," and "What Barbara Told Us."

What Haunts Me

"For a Taxi Driver Named Comfort" was anthologized in *Waiting Room Reader, Vol. 2: Words to Keep You Company*, published by CavanKerry Press. "Naming the Bones" was anthologized in *Letters to the World*, published by Red Hen Press.

I'm very grateful to the writers and friends who have cheered me on and/or inspired me to keep writing, particularly: Cynthia Marie Hoffman, Sarah Kain Gutowski, Steph DePrez, Cecilia Gigliotti, Elle Carroll, and Sabine Lutz. Sincere thanks also to my family, who've encouraged my writing since I was a tween imitating Carolyn Keene. Above all, I'd like to especially acknowledge Peter and Frida for their ever-present support and love, which sustains me more than I can express. Last but not least, love and thanks to all the cats and dogs in my life who've accompanied me so loyally over the decades.

About the Author

Bernadette Geyer is the author of *The Scabbard of Her Throat* and editor of *My Cruel Invention: A Contemporary Poetry Anthology*. A writer of poetry and prose, her works have appeared widely in publications including *Bennington Review, Salamander, Barrow Street, Oxford American, Westerly,* and elsewhere. A long-time resident of Northern Virginia, Geyer now lives in Berlin, Germany, where she moved with her family in 2013. Her translations of poems by German writers have been published in *Asymptote* and *The Massachusetts Review*.

About the Author

Similar April Gloaming Titles

All Things Holy and Heathen
Chelsea C. Jackson

She Used to Be on a Milk Carton
Kailey Tedesco

Aria Viscera
Kristi Carter

The Eaten
Leah Saint Marie

Dear Excavator
Evan D. Williams

Ash Tuesday
Ariadne Blayde

APRIL GLOAMING

View our full catalogue at aprilgloaming.com